Feeling Crispy?

A Guide to Burnout Recovery

Kate Steiner, Ph.D.

This book is dedicated to my biggest cheerleaders, Mom, Dad, Jeremy, Josie, Suzanne, and the ZFG crew.

Contents

Introduction

I am so grateful that you have found your way to this book. I remember so clearly the day I defended my dissertation, which included the model presented in Chapter Two. My committee members were so clear that I could not let the work sit on a shelf that it had to be shared with the world. Four years later, I am sharing it with all of you.

After implementing the model in my own life, I am much happier and more resilient to the experience of Burnout, and I want that experience for everyone around me. This is a practice that I employ daily, and four years later, I am still learning about myself and what best supports me in moments of Burnout Recovery. Be patient with yourself as you start this process; it is not meant to be an overnight journey. Instead, this is a new way of living your life.

As you read, I hope that you will take time to reflect, journal, process, and experiment. I was intentional in making this e-book a short read. I wanted to offer a resource that people could use when they were already feeling overwhelmed, and even reading something that could help feels like a burden.

I hope you return to this book as a continued resource as your journey to Burnout Recovery progresses, shifts, and changes. Now, let's get started because I know you are Feeling Crispy.

Chapter One

Feeling Crispy

*"Burnout is what happens when you try
to avoid being human for too long."*
—Michael Gungor

I did not realize that I was a crispy overcooked turkey. Perhaps you've seen the classic comedy movie Christmas Vacation and remember the Christmas dinner scene when Clark cuts into the turkey. On the outside, it looked perfectly cooked. But once cut into, it explodes into an overcooked, overdone crispy, crispy bird. Nothing is left but that crispy, crispy skin. With the escape of steam, the family realizes that it was just in the oven for too long. That's how I felt when I reached my total burnout point a few years ago.

1

Feeling Crispy is how I now define my Burnout. When I am working so hard to maintain that vision of perfection on the outside. I am using all my energy to hold it together. On the inside, I am a hot, steamy mess—feeling all the emotions of anger or sadness, nothing beyond those two feelings. And if you were to cut just under my skin, I would explode, and that hot, steamy mess would all come rushing out.

So, are you Feeling Crispy? My guess is yes because you are here. Welcome, friend; we are all Feeling Crispy together. We all have behaviors that showcase our crispy feelings to others. They can be hard to hide, especially those who know us best.

Crispy behaviors are when we reach our breaking point following a burn event. You may feel fatigued, unmotivated, and irritated. The behaviors or outward showing of our emotions can look different for every person. The present in different ways and impact us physically, emotionally, and socially.

Think about your Crispy behaviors; what indicators tell you that you have reached the end of your rope? Do you self-isolate? Are you short-tempered? Do you become very quiet and withdrawn? Do other people withdraw from you? If you found yourself saying check, check, and check, you are in the right place, and this is just the right book for you at this time.

We all have times when we are feeling crispy. Crispy feelings and behaviors are okay; they are indicators that we are out of balance and have strayed from our centering point. We can use crispy behaviors as warning signs that we have been grinding ourselves just a little too hard. Crispy behaviors are indicators that our stress reaction is occurring at full force. Our ability to process rational thoughts leaves us, and we revert into the body to keep ourselves safe. Our fight or flight will kick in, and therefore people who are Feeling Crispy are reactive, angry, withdrawn, or irritated.

Professionals who are Feeling Crispy may also experience insomnia, lack of enthusiasm, and feelings of ineffectiveness. They may be susceptible to an increase in the use of drugs and alcohol, as well. Burnout can also increase personal relationship problems among professionals' friends and family members. Maslach, Jackson, and Leiter identified three components of burnout as part of the Maslach Burnout Inventory: General Survey (MBI-GS); these include emotional exhaustion, cynicism, and professional efficacy. Emotional exhaustion develops as an individual's emotions are drained, and it is often described as fatigue, worn-out, a loss of energy, or depletion. Others may observe professionals suffering from exhaustion as having low energy. Colleagues, friends and family may report that you are more disconnected from them and the work during your crispy moments. Cynicism presents as a reflection of indifference or a distant attitude toward work. This is different from setting a boundary for professionalism at work, but rather when you experience cynicism, you do not care if your work is done poorly.

Feeling Crispy happens when we experience burn events. Burn events are experiences, activities, events, and interactions with other humans that cause us to feel drained, exhausted, and overwhelmed. There are two types of burn events, expected and unexpected. Expected burn events are those that we can look at our calendar and know that they are about to happen. They can include a long work week where we need to be available on the evenings or weekends, a meeting with a complicated human, even family gatherings can present as an expected burn event. Unexpected events were those that occurred without warning. Unexpected burn events may also hit harder, as these are things that we may not be ready for, such as learning about the death of a loved one, a challenging medical diagnosis, a break-up, or even having additional work dropped on us when we are already overwhelmed. I will cover how we can better prepare and recover from these burn events in the following chapters.

For now, we must recognize that these events are expected for all humans, so the concept that burnout can be avoided is crap. While we cannot avoid it, we can better identify burnout. We can employ better preparation plans and implement a continuous recovery plan integrated into our lives. By the end of this book, you will be able to identify a solid recovery plan that will increase your resilience to burn event experiences.

Chapter Two

The Steiner Self-Reflection Sustainability and Wellness Model

"The more stress you accumulate, the heavier it becomes. If you accumulate too much, the weight of carrying it can break you."

—Oscar Auliq-Ice

We know that we are Feeling Crispy, so how do we go from there to a place of Burnout Recovery?

Fun fact as humans, we approach our Burnout Recovery in very similar ways from person to person. This model was created by analyzing the interviews from several professionals and continues to be informed and updated by

my one-on-one work with clients. I am excited to introduce you to the Steiner Self-Reflection Sustainability and
Wellness Model (SSRSW).

Steiner Self-Reflection Sustainability & Wellness Model

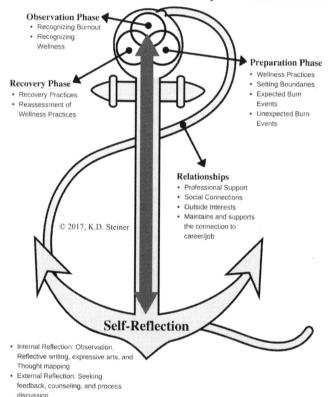

Observation Phase
- Recognizing Burnout
- Recognizing Wellness

Preparation Phase
- Wellness Practices
- Setting Boundaries
- Expected Burn Events
- Unexpected Burn Events

Recovery Phase
- Recovery Practices
- Reassessment of Wellness Practices

Relationships
- Professional Support
- Social Connections
- Outside Interests
- Maintains and supports the connection to career/job

© 2017, K.D. Steiner

Self-Reflection
- Internal Reflection: Observation, Reflective writing, expressive arts, and Thought mapping
- External Reflection: Seeking feedback, counseling, and process discussion

The Steiner Self-Reflection Sustainability and Wellness
model consists of three phases: Observation, Preparation,
and Recovery. Each stage is connected to the others but

does not function in a linear pattern, and more than one phase may be happening simultaneously. The whole process is anchored in self-reflection and supported by outside interests. This chapter will serve as an introduction to each phase, with the following chapters digging deeper into each and how you can implement each into your life.

Observation Phase

The Observation Phase requires self-reflection from you. During this phase, you note what burnout looks like for you and times that burnout is more likely to occur. This is the phase where you identify your expected burn events and notice your unexpected burn events. This is less of a step and more of a constant, meaning that as you observe and identify your Burn Events and Burnout, you will start to develop habits and rituals, and the observation will become a natural experience for you. You may find yourself completing a calendar review every week or taking note of your burn events at the end of each workday.

Preparation Phase

Burnout is often approached as something to be avoided rather than a state of mind to prepare for by embracing it as a natural experience. I have found in my research that many people approach burnout as an experience to prepare for; by highlighting critical times in their workspace that they knew were busier than other times. Preparation also includes preventative care for our physical and mental wellbeing. This phase is closely related to the recovery phase. When you are in Preparation, you need to plan how you will recover specifically from busy times and burn events as they occur.

Recovery Phase

The recovery phase may occur following an expected burn event that you prepared for or after an unexpected burn event. This phase is most notable as a period of reflection and centering. You will likely move quickly from this phase into the observation or preparation phases. A key element to this phase is the practice of spending time away from work. This may include taking a vacation, using sick time, or using flextime. This is also highlighted by setting boundaries between your workspace and other spaces in your life by establishing rituals to allow you to leave work at the workspace. This time away should be planned, in advance or enacted when you feel at a breaking point in your burnout experience.

Relationships

Relationships help us maintain our connection to our work and life in general. They can play both supportive and harmful roles in our burnout recovery. Essentially, we cannot wholly avoid having other people impact us. It is essential to name the positive relationships you have, such as supportive colleagues, mentors, friends, and those that negatively affect you.

Self-Reflection

Each of the three phases is anchored in the process of self-reflection. You must know yourself to find recovery for yourself. Self-reflection can occur in several ways; it can be internal through thinking, journaling, pondering, etc., or external by sharing your thoughts and musings with someone else or speaking to them aloud.

Ready to learn more about each phase? Let's dig in!

Chapter Three

Identifying Burnout – The Observation Phase

"Burnout, like any difficult experience,
is a great teacher. My question is:
What is it trying to tell you?"

—Dr. Rebecca Ray

Feeling Crispy is just one indicator we can use to identify our burnout. One of the main reasons so many of us experience full-on burnout instead of catching it after each Burn Event is that we have conditioned that this experience is just how it should be. That comes with our chosen career path and successful people continue to push through without recovery. The more data we can gather regarding our burnout responses, the better we can recognize when we are on the road to burn city and take an exit to recovery faster. Recognition is the first step to finding recovery and reclaiming our joy. So, what else do we need to be on the lookout for?

While we all experience burnout differently, I want you to reflect on how each of these shared experiences presents for you as you read this chapter. Please put on your reflection cap; we are diving in deep!

Burnout shows up in our bodies in two main ways: physically and emotionally. While your experience may be different, there are some common ways to recognize burnout quicker. Let's start with how burnout may impact you physically.

Have you ever had a day like this? You wake up and are immediately greeted with a headache. You swing your feet off the bed, and your body feels heavy and stiff. You make your way to the kitchen, and you have no appetite and feel a bit nauseous. You make some coffee or tea and try to think about the day before you, but your thoughts are a little jumbled, and you are having trouble focusing. You start to wonder if you are coming down with something. You know you didn't sleep well the night before, which will impact your day. You keep moving through the morning and your day, and everything feels like it is either going too fast, at warp speed, or too slow. You finally get to bed at the end of the night and have difficulty settling your thoughts. You feel restless and end up tossing and turning for another night.

Not a great day, right? How many times have you had a day like this? Likely you've had more than one in a row. Each of those experiences or symptoms could result from something else but combined, and they are a good indicator that you are feeling burnt out and need to start recovery planning and action now.

What about the emotional side? Let's take that same day, and in addition to feeling physically unwell, you also experience being more sensitive emotionally. A meeting with your boss that generally would not have upset left you holding back tears. Something your partner said flared your hurt and anger. You used to love going to work, and now you dread it, feeling worse and worse as you get closer to the day's start time. For some reason, you experience more anxiety, and yesterday you are pretty sure you had your first ever panic attack.

Here are two checklists for you to use to assess how burnout is showing up for you.

> ➤ Physical Burnout Checklist
> ➤ Headaches
> ➤ Fatigue
> ➤ Difficulty Concentrating
> ➤ Stomach issues
> ➤ Difficulty falling asleep or staying asleep
> ➤ Difficulty waking
> ➤ Body Aches

Emotional Burnout Checklist

> ➤ Sadness for unknown reasons
> ➤ Anger for unknown reasons
> ➤ Increased anxiety
> ➤ Feeling more raw

Burn Events versus Burnout

Did you see the term "Burn Events" earlier in this chapter and think, "what the heck are those? I've never heard of them!" Well, dear friends, let me tell you now.

Burn Events are what happens to us before Burnout. They are what create your full-on burnout experience. Burn Events are circumstances, activities, interactions, and happenings in our life that leave us feeling overwhelmed, fatigued, and emotionally drained. If you are thinking, "Thanks for describing most days, Dr. Kate," then you are on the right track because these occur daily. They can range from a tough meeting to a week of many extra hours to interacting with a problematic human (I know you just pictured someone!). Knowing and understanding our Burn Events is vital because when we do not recover from them as they happen, they will compound, snowball, and lead to full-on burnout.

Picture it this way. You have a tough week at work, working long hours and into most of your evenings, and you push through waiting for the weekend to have a little downtime. You make it to the weekend, and your partner reminds you there are plans to visit with their parents this weekend. Generally, you enjoy those visits, but you were looking forward to having a low-key, relaxing, and restful weekend. You do not want to disappoint your partner, so you push through the visit. While on the way, you end up sitting in traffic for hours because of an accident on the road. You finally arrive and are met at the door by your partner's aunt, your least favorite person in the family, and she immediately starts asking about work, stating that she can't believe that they pay people to do your job. You enjoy parts of the visit and head home only to sit in traffic again, finally arriving home. You remember still needing to do laundry and prep for the week ahead. You wake up on Monday already feeling behind.

Do you see how this push-through cycle can become burnout very quickly?

Beyond how Burnout shows up for us physically and emotionally, we also want to consider how our experience with Burnout impacts people around us. For this I like to use the acronym C.O.P.E.

Consider: This includes how Burnout shows up for us in our bodies and minds. It also includes how we show up in our worlds when we are experiencing a Burn Event or are in a state of Burnout.

Obtain Feedback: Sometimes, we do not know how we impact other people when we are in a stressed state of mind. By asking the people who care about us for feedback, we can discover behaviors we were unaware of.

Patterns: Now that you are more familiar with Burn Events, we want to start paying attention to them and when and how they occur. Are there patterns for your Burn Events? Do they happen in a specific place? Is a particular person always involved? Have you found a particular time of the day to be more challenging? We can better address Burn Events through the Preparation Phase which is covered in the next chapter when we know these patterns.

Examine: Finally, we want to examine the behaviors of other people. Observing what they do when we think they are stressed can give us insight by reflecting on whether that is also how we show up when overwhelmed. You may notice that a co-worker becomes very quiet when they seem overwhelmed, or you have a friend who amps up when stressed. Might these be behaviors you also exhibit?

Once we know more about ourselves and how our Burnout presents in our bodies, minds, and the world, we can better address Feeling Crispy through the Preparation Phase.

Chapter Four

The Preparation Phase

"Balance is not better time management, but better boundary management. Balance means making choices and enjoying those choices."
—Betsy Jacobson

Preparation may sound a little like a recipe to avoid burn-out, which you may recall we can't do. Perhaps it is a different way of thinking about Burn Events and Burnout. I covered how some burn events are things that we can expect. We can look at our calendar and identify those times and experiences before they happen. The Preparation Phase focuses on creating a plan for just those times.

Think back to when you knew that you would have a hectic workweek. You knew that you would put in longer hours or have a higher emotional demand on you, and your energy would be more drained. Have you ever approached those times with a plan for how you would face the week? That's preparation.

Preparation includes the following things, planning for upcoming expected burn events, setting boundaries and non-negotiables, maintaining general well-being and wellness, and preventative care. This chapter will focus on preparing for forthcoming Burn Events and preventive care. At the same time, boundaries and non-negotiables will be covered entirely in chapter five, and maintaining wellness practices will be covered in chapter six.

In the last chapter, the concept of Burn Events was introduced. Identifying and observing those events is so important to prepare for them differently. Let's think about how you might approach your calendar differently by highlighting the upcoming Burn Events.

When I look at my calendar for the week ahead, I mark which days will include Expected Burn Events. As I write this, I am traveling to a conference to present burnout and support attendees in their Burnout Recovery. This is a Burn Event for me. I love to travel, but I also know it takes a toll on my overall wellness. I don't eat, exercise, sleep, or recover like I do at home. But it also serves as a recovery point because I am doing work I love, interacting with friends old and new, and socializing. When I looked at this week's travel schedule, I knew I needed to put a few things into place to show up as my best self every day of the conference. (Side note: Your best self looks different every day!)

Showing up as my Best Self meant I needed to get to bed a little earlier the day before my travels. It also meant that I needed to increase my water intake that day and intentionally drink water while I traveled on the plane. I packed snacks so that no poor soul would experience my hanger, and I have long ago given up the idea of fashion for comfort while traveling, so tennis shoes are my favorite travel buddies. This is one example of preparing for a Burn Event.

Let's take a look at your calendar next week.... go ahead and pull it up right now... I'll wait…

Great! Now I want you to look at next week and mark anything that would be a Burn Event for you. Remember, a Burn Event is anything that will lead you to feel overwhelmed, emotionally drained, or fatigued following that event. It could be a meeting with someone you find frustrating, a big deadline looming, a family gathering, a long workday, or, like in my case, today's travel.

Once you've marked your Burn Events, I want you to think about the things you need in your life to show up as your Best Self each day. Is it your morning routine, first cup of coffee, journaling, exercise, affirmations, or a combo of the above? What do you need throughout the day to continue to be at your best? How might you recover from those Burn Events? The answers to these questions signify what you need to put into place for your Preparation for Burn Events. Why? Because when we get overwhelmed, these practices are often the first things that get cut when they should be the last.

Okay, so you have named your Burn Events and are on your way to creating a plan to prepare them before they happen and while they happen. However, you also want to have a plan in place for after they happen. This is a planned and intentional recovery, and it is an integral part of the Preparation Phase. Look back at your calendar and schedule in time to rest and recoup after each Burn Event. It could be at the end of the day, the start of the next day, or a 5 -10 minute break right after that frustrating meeting. I will share more on specific ways to recover in Chapter Seven. Right now, I want you to focus on scheduling that time for yourself.

This intentional recovery space is an essential part of the process. You have to give yourself this time and treat it as if it is with the most crucial person in your life because it is with the most crucial person in your life. You!

Speaking of you, let's talk about one essential part of the Preparation Phase, preventative care. Really, Dr. Kate, preventive care? Yes, dear reader. Preventative care is a significant aspect of this phase because it is almost impossible to be the happiest, healthiest version of yourself if you are not healthy. So, keeping up with your physical and mental preventative care is essential.

Physical Preventative Care: This includes those annual physical exams with your healthcare provider, precancer screenings, vaccinations, and anything you do for your physical wellness. Having a solid understanding of your physical body and recognizing when things do not feel right is essential for observing and identifying your burnout and recovering from your burnout.

Mental Preventative Care: Raise your hand if you think that seeing a counselor, therapist, coach, or the equivalent should only happen when you are having a hard time or are feeling depressed. Most of us believe this, and I'm here to tell you that you can benefit greatly from seeing a professional when things are going well as prevention for those tough times. I use coaches for my business, physical health, and mental health to develop better skills to employ when I need them. I recommend seeing a professional for your mental health at least a couple of times a year to develop different coping skills. This also means that you have a relationship with a professional already established for a time when you may need them regularly.

The two final pieces of the Preparation phase are setting boundaries and establishing our wellness practices. The following two chapters focus specifically on these areas. Now let's dig into Boundary Setting.

Chapter Five

Setting Boundaries

"You are not required to set yourself on fire to keep other people warm."
—Unknown

As we continue to discover the Preparation Phase, this chapter will cover essential aspects in creating our healthiest, happiest spaces: setting boundaries and work standards. Let's start with setting boundaries.

I once had a supervisor whom I seemed unable to please. I remember sitting through an evaluation on the verge of tears as they proceeded to tell me all the things I had gotten wrong in my job over the last 6-months. I held my breath as they brought up a mistake that had happened months before, an instance I barely remembered and one they had never mentioned before. I remember thinking, "Why didn't you just tell me?" It was a terrible meeting, and I left still not knowing exactly what they expected of me in my role in the organization. I believed there wasn't anything I could do right in working with this person. Every day after that, I felt like I was a disappointment at work.

Have you ever had someone come to you disappointed because you did not reach their expectations of you, all the while you never knew what they wanted in the first place?

Setting boundaries is vital for maintaining a healthy space at work; they are also a critical way to teach other people how we expect them to treat us. Consider the expectations you have of other people. Now, think about how many people around you know your expectations. If you are like most of us, you have some people who have not been informed, and thus with them, you will always end up with an unmet expectation or be disappointed in your interactions with them.

Boundaries are the communicated expectations of other people to support us in creating a space where we can show up as our best selves. There are several types of boundaries that we want to consider as we evaluate what we need from others; physical, emotional, mental, time, and

Physical Boundaries

Our physical boundaries include our needs for physical space, comfort with touch, and physical needs like rest, eating, sleeping, and drinking water. So being able to tell people, "I'm really sorry. But I need to take a few minutes to eat, or I will get angry with you." That may or may not have been a boundary I have set on multiple occasions. It happens. It's letting someone know you're about to go hangry if you don't stop and get something to eat, or "I'm not really a hugging person, but I would be fine with a fist bump to say hello." You are offering that space again to set your expectation.

Emotional Boundaries

Our emotional boundaries define what you need regarding having your feelings respected and honored. To set emotional boundaries, you need to understand how much you can take from another person emotionally, know when to share or not share your emotions, and limit emotional sharing to those who respond poorly. So, this might sound something to the effect of, "I'm so sorry you're having such a tough time. Right now, I'm not in a place to take in all of this information. Do you think we can come back to this conversation later?"

Time Boundaries

Our boundary of time concerns your time and energy. Remember that your time and energy are precious. It is one of our most valuable resources, it is the one that is finite, and beyond prioritizing, we cannot create more time. It is so crucial that you protect how it's utilized. This is important at home, work, and in our social settings. You have to understand your priorities to set time boundaries. You need to assess your priorities and set aside enough time for all the areas of your life without over-committing. Setting a limit here might sound like something to be effective. "I would love to help, but I would be over-committing myself, which would not be fair to you."

Mental Boundaries

Mental boundaries refer to your mental and intellectual capacity. This includes your thoughts, ideas, curiosity, respectfulness, and willingness to dialogue and understand important here. When we are fatigued, our capacity to discuss can be significantly impacted. Time and space also come into are also a factor here. This is about your best workday; picture it from start to end. How did your day start, what were you able to accomplish, and during what times of the day did those accomplishments happen? We all have a natural ebb and flow for our mental capacity. I find myself doing my best work between 10 am and 2 pm. After 2 pm, I have less focus available for projects or writing. Still, I gain energy from meeting with other people during that time frame until about 7 pm, and I usually have a creative spark early in the morning before 8 am. What does your mental flow look like? Are there ways that you can better utilize those naturally motivated times? Setting a boundary here might sound like I would love to talk about this more, but I don't have the mental capacity to discuss this right now, and I want to be my best for this conversation. Are you free later today or first thing tomorrow morning?

Setting Work Standards

In addition to setting boundaries with other humans, it is also essential that we establish expectations for ourselves in the workspace. I call these work standards. These are your own set of standards of excellence. They are clear guidelines that help you establish the time and space to have a most successful workday and have a sense of harmony between your work and the rest of your life.

Consider what you need daily to show up fully and be as present as possible during the workday. For myself, that includes a clearly defined and consistent start time and an end time for the day. You want to establish habits and routines that support you in quickly achieving your work standards. Here are a few things you should consider when drafting your expectations.

Your Opening Routine

What will your opening routine look like? Regardless of the work you do, consider starting your day as though you are opening a shop or restaurant. When you open a service-based business, there is always a checklist of tasks that support you in having everything you will need ready to go when the sign is flipped from closed to open. I remember working in a restaurant, and the task list looked something like this:

- ➢ Brew Coffee and Iced Tea
- ➢ Get water carafes ready
- ➢ Prep the salad-making area in the kitchen
- ➢ Turn on all the lights
- ➢ Check that all the tables have silverware set
- ➢ Wipe down all menus

> ➤ Write out the specials menu on the front chalkboard
> ➤ Unlock the front doors promptly at 11 am

Going through this routine meant that both the business and I were ready for the lunch rush. Even if you work in an office, you need to have an opening routine that helps signal to your brain that you are transitioning into work mode. Think about how you open your office and turn on your computer. What are the first tasks you complete? Do you always go straight to email? Is there another way to start your day that would be more helpful, like creating a priority list for the day and then starting on the most challenging task first?

Managing Interruptions

Sometimes interruptions are a part of our work and need to be welcomed, and sometimes we need to limit them to focus more on the task at hand. To start thinking about your standards in managing interruptions, start by identifying them. What kind of interruptions do you have throughout the day? Include anything that takes your focus from your work. What notifications have you set up that draw your attention away, like email, social media, phone, slack, direct messages, the phone ringing, people stopping by your space, etc.? Write them all down. Once you have that list, please take a little bit of time to consider each of these needs to be an interruption, meaning is it something you need to attend to the moment you receive the notification? If they can wait, how would it feel to turn off the alert or use certain times throughout your day to work without those interruptions? What expectations do you need to put in place to create that space each workday?

One of my standards that creates interruption-free space is using the Pomodoro method twice daily. I chose a project that I needed uninterrupted focus to complete; I will set a timer for 25 minutes and focus only on that task during that time. It could be responding to emails, writing content for my upcoming course, or working on a report for a client, but it is the only thing that it opens on my computer desktop. No other windows or tabs, my phone is on do not disturb, and my office door is closed if needed. If I listen to music, there are no lyrics. I love using movie scores during this work time. I work on the task for the entire 25 minutes, and then when the timing goes off, I take a 5-minute break (usually to have a dance party.) After the break, I can start another 25-minute work block and work more freely by allowing interruptions.

Priority Setting

To wisely use the time and space without interruptions, you need to identify the projects and tasks best suited for those timeframes. This is where considering and setting our daily priorities can be helpful. Creating a "to-do" list is overwhelming because it almost always includes more work than I can get done in one workday. I have had tremendous success in creating a priority list. This list contains only the things that are a priority for me to finish that day, and it is limited to no more than three things. I know how you can get everything done if you only put three items on the list every day! These are also the things that I find myself procrastinating most often. When I put off these projects for more straightforward or enjoyable tasks, I do not feel accomplished at the end of the day. Even if I did much work, in my heart, I know that I did not get the most important task finished.

Setting the priority to complete these two to three things and accomplishing that by using my interruption-free time, I feel much more accomplished and less anxious at the end of the day. How often would you say that your day is consumed by busy work, and you end your day feeling like you didn't have time to focus on the big picture items? Using a priority list can help you stay focused on those more significant projects because you actively and intentionally create time and space. I also recommend that you start your day with one of these tasks during a stretch of uninterrupted time before you get into responding to emails and other reaction-based work.

Closing Routine

Like your opening routine, your closing routine signals to your body and mind that you are transitioning away from the workspace into other areas of your life. Many people also use this time to set themselves up for success the next day. Let's return to my time working in a restaurant and the general tasks I remember about the closing shift.

- ➢ Clean all tables
- ➢ Sweep and mop floors in the dining area and sever prep spaces
- ➢ Closeout and reconcile the cash register
- ➢ Put cash for the next day into the safe, close, and lock
- ➢ Clean the salad station, fill containers, and cover all containers in plastic wrap
- ➢ Prep coffee and tea maker for the next day
- ➢ Fill salt and pepper shakers

> Fill and put away ketchup bottles
> Prep silverware in napkins
> Empty all garbage cans and take the trash out to the dumpster
> Turn off all lights
> Lock door

What would you include if you were to write out your closing routine? What tasks would help you entirely shut down for the day and be able to show up tomorrow with a prepped and ready-to-go workstation? You might start by shutting down your computer, cleaning up files on your desk, and creating a priority list for the next day. Think about what you must complete to truly leave work at work for the day.

Non-Work Hours Expectations

You now have a plan for starting your workday, managing your interruptions, creating priority tasks to fill that uninterrupted time, and closing out your workday to transition into the rest of your life. But what about when work shows up while you live the rest of your life? These are your work standards for your non-work time. The boundaries you set for yourself to show up fully for yourself and the people around you when you are not at work.

These look very different for every person and can be impacted by your career field, specific expectations from your boss, and where you are in your life or career. Early on in my career, I was much more available during non-work hours in good part due to my desire to prove myself on the job as being dependable. Over the years, that definition changed as I became more secure with myself and my work.

To consider your own non-work hours' expectations, let's start with the idea of accessibility. What does it mean to you to be "accessible" for work at this point in your career? Do you check your email during the weekend but never respond? Do you not check your email but respond to a call or text message from your supervisor during non-work hours? Do you not answer or react to anything related to work during your non-work time? Because this can vary so greatly from person to person, you need to first consider the expectations, both spoken and unspoken, from your place of work. Do you agree with these expectations? What are your needs for personal space and time away from work? Is there a balance or harmony that can be found if these expectations do not align with each other?

Once you have a better framework around these work standards, you also want to consider establishing these as a boundary. It is helpful to communicate your work standards to the humans you work with daily. This helps them understand you better, enabling you to be more accountable to your expectations.

You may want to return to this chapter after reading Chapter Six about the 6 Important Areas of Wellness, as you may want to include them as part of your boundaries and work standards.

The Six Important Areas of Wellness

"Self-care is giving yourself permission to pause."
—Cecilia Tran

Wellness and these six areas of wellness are ever-present in the SSRSW Model. Wellness is part of the Observation Phase as we identify which wellness areas we focus on and those we lack. It plays a significant role in the Preparation Phase as we use our sites of Wellness to create our plans in approaching our Expected Burn Events. Having general wellness practices helps us be more resilient to those Unexpected Burn Events. Finally, we use these areas of Wellness during the Recovery Phase to support our journey back to our happiest, healthiest selves. This chapter will highlight all six areas and help you reflect on how to address each in your life.

Picture a wheel with six spokes. Each of these spokes represents an important wellness area that impacts our ability to be our best selves daily: the Physical, Social, Emotional, Financial, Intellectual, and Spiritual areas. I have found both for myself and in working with clients that we want to approach our wheel by giving equal parts to each spoke. Based on our greatest needs, we naturally shift around these wellness areas as humans. This means that at least one area may be left out, creating a flat tire effect.

About a year ago, I worked in a town about a 40-minute drive from where I lived. One day, a light appeared in the center console during my commute home. I was indicating low tire pressure in the front driver's side tire. I took the next exit and parked at the gas station; sure enough, the tire was completely flat. I still had about 20 miles on the trip because I was nervous about getting home. I was not thinking clearly, so I did not think to call for help through the roadside service my car insurance company offers; I did not think about getting help changing the tire to the spare; I only wanted to get home. Thinking that maybe the one tire had just lost all its air, I filled it up and continued my journey. I stopped twice more on the way home to fill up the tire. I made it home, and the next day when I took the car in to have the tire looked at, it was clear that it needed to be replaced. Though it wasn't long, I continued to drive on that flat tire, and I could have damaged my car or gotten into an accident with that choice.

Our wellness is much like that tire. When we do not focus on all six areas, we create a flat tire in areas we are not considering. As I did on my drive home, you can drive on a flat tire, but it is slower. It may be a bumpier drive, and eventually, we will damage the vehicle (you) if we do not fix the tire. As you read through the definitions for each of the six areas, consider where is your flat tire right now.

Physical Wellness

Our Physical Wellness includes anything that is connected to our physical body. You want to consider how you move your body and what you put into your body, like food, water, alcohol, or other substances. Our sleep impacts multiple wellness areas and is considered a part of our Physical Wellness. You want to consider the amount of sleep you get and the quality of sleep. When you think about your current Physical Wellness, what thoughts come up? Is this one of your flat tire areas?

When we think about improving our Physical Wellness, people often start by thinking about their exercise routines and eating. You can use the following reflection prompts to consider where you might focus on your Physical Wellness.

➤ Are you eating a balanced, nutritional diet? What do your eating habits look like?
➤ How would you define your exercise routine?
➤ How many glasses of water are you drinking each day?
➤ Are you generally free from illness?
➤ Do you schedule and attend annual check-ups and follow-ups as prescribed, including dental appointments?
➤ How many hours of sleep are you getting on average per night?
➤ How would you describe your bedtime routine? Do you have a consistent wake-up time?
➤ If at all, do you use tobacco, alcohol, or prescribed drugs responsibly and moderately?

Social Wellness

Our Social Wellness includes how we interact with other humans. Humans are social animals, and we function best when we are pack members, similar to all other mammals. We want to think about our interactions with other people for our Social Wellness. This also includes our ability to resolve conflicts, set boundaries, and respond to the needs of others. This area is heavily impacted when we are forced into isolation for any reason. Consider the following reflection questions to see if this might currently be a flat tire area for you.

> Do you have at least three people with whom you have a close and trusting relationship?
> Are you able to resolve conflicts in all areas of your life?
> How would you describe a satisfying social interaction? When was the last time you experienced that kind of interaction?
> Are you aware and able to set/respect your boundaries and those set by others?
> What is a group or organization where you experience a sense of belonging?
> What is your favorite way to engage with others socially?

Financial Wellness

Financial Wellness is our relationship to money. This includes our ability to make and be responsible for our financial decisions. You may consider how you approach savings, retirement, credit cards, and other debt here. Financial Wellness is an area that many of us do not think about as often as we consider our physical or emotional wellness. Yet, this area can significantly impact us in all the other areas of wellness in our lives. We mustn't ignore it. The following reflection questions will support you in accessing if this is a flat tire area for you.

- ➤ How do you live within your means and take responsibility for your financial decisions?
- ➤ Describe your spending and saving values and habits. Do they align?
- ➤ In what ways do you actively plan for periods in your life when you may not have an income?
- ➤ How do you approach paying your bills and managing credit?
- ➤ In what ways do you balance present-day spending with future savings?
- ➤ How do your financial beliefs align with the closest people (family, partner, children, close friends)?

Emotional Wellness

Emotional Wellness is our connection and interaction with our feelings. This includes honoring our range of emotions, from our ability to self-comfort or self-console when we are upset or overwhelmed to our sense of humor and use of laughter. It includes our definition of emotions. Also, our views and emotions we share with others and keep to ourselves. You may also consider which other areas of wellness you utilize to tap into your emotional wellness. Are they easier to access when talking to a friend? What about when you work out or spend time in nature? The following reflection questions will help you consider how this might be a flat tire area.

- ➤ How would you describe your sense of control in your life?
- ➤ How do you approach change in your life?
- ➤ When you have a problem, do you consider it an area of growth or a challenge to overcome?
- ➤ Describe your sense of humor and ability to laugh at yourself.
- ➤ How do you comfort and console yourself when you feel upset or overwhelmed?
- ➤ What role does responsibility play for you regarding your feelings and how you express them?

Intellectual Wellness

Intellectual Wellness addresses how we expand our minds, learn, and grow within our thought patterns. This area also addresses how we define our thoughts as either positive, negative, or neutral. Our career satisfaction is present here because boredom can lead to Burn Events and Burnout if we are not connected intellectually. The time we commit to professional development is an aspect of our Intellectual Wellness. Might this be a flat tire area? Use the following reflection questions to assess your Intellectual Wellness.

- ➢ What new skills and information are you currently learning?
- ➢ Would you consider most of your thoughts positive, negative, or neutral?
- ➢ How satisfied are you with your current career area?
- ➢ Describe how you commit time and energy to professional growth and self-development.
- ➢ In what ways do you pursue mentally stimulating interests or hobbies?

Spiritual Wellness

Spiritual Wellness is our connection to something greater than ourselves. For many people, this comes into play through religious practice. It might be through prayer, yoga, a connection to nature, getting out in nature, or the universe in general. For some people, it's a connection to science. This is the area of wellness that gives address our sense of meaning and purpose in life. It encompasses our faith and impacts how we see the world. The following reflection questions will help you consider if this is a flat tire area for you.

> ➤ Describe your sense of meaning or purpose in life.
> ➤ Are you happy with the beliefs and values you hold? Why or why not?
> ➤ How do you engage in reflective growth? (Through prayer, meditation, etc.)
> ➤ Describe your ability to forgive yourself and others.
> ➤ What are the principles/values/ethics that guide your life? How connected do you feel to them right now?

Our flat tire areas change over time based on what might be happening in our lives. It is essential to return to these reflection questions when we notice the impact of a flat tire.

How do we manage the flat tire effect daily? Through maintaining our general and daily wellness practices. Adjusting your daily routines does not have to be a huge undertaking. There are ways to make minor adjustments that will benefit you greatly. Let's think about this for each area starting with Physical Wellness. Think about how you are moving your body each day. Do you track your steps? Do you utilize a step goal for that? What about how you fuel your body with food and water? Do you ensure that you get enough water throughout the day? Is the food you eat giving you the nutrition and energy you need? Think about your sleep cycle. What changes could you make to your wind-down or morning routine that would support you getting enough rest?

Moving on to the Social Wellness area. What are you doing for your social wellness daily? Is there someone you talk to daily to share what's been going on, any frustrations you're having, or any joys or wins you're having? Where does your social engagement come from every day? Consider what may be some small ways that you could increase your social wellness. If you want to move your body more, you could join a group fitness class that would benefit you socially. Sometimes including activities that have you simply sharing space with other humans can significantly impact your wellness in this area.

When I think about daily practices for Financial Wellness, I can feel a little overwhelmed. Instead, I think about impacting my financial wellness every week. Each week, I have a scheduled timeframe to look at my personal and business budgets. I spend that time balancing my present-day spending with saving for the future and considering my upcoming large purchases. I reflect on what I might need for emergencies. Simply put, I spend intentional time with my finances instead of opening up my bank app and hoping there is money in the account.

Let's consider how we can impact our Intellectual Wellness through daily routines. What are some ways that you can learn new skills throughout your day? It might be a routine of reading the news or a news email covering several headlines and stories. Maybe you add a quick logic game to your lunch break. When commuting daily, I started listening to a podcast or audiobook on my way home every day. This practice helped me unwind from the workday and learn more about something I found interesting.

For Spiritual Wellness, consider adding a gratitude practice to your day to write down what you're thankful for. Make sure that you include yourself on that list. At the end of each day, maybe you have a reflection and a journal practice. One of the things that I have added to my morning routine is a post-it note on my mirror, and I read it while I brush my teeth. I'm going to be brushing my teeth. Instead of creating time for another practice, I added something to a habit I already have, supporting how I show up for the day. The note is pretty simple. It reads, "I am joyful. I am calm. I show respect to every living thing. I do my work honestly. I live with an attitude of gratitude."

Instead of creating new spaces for your wellness, think about some small ways to include those aspects into habits you already have in your daily life. As we review each of the six areas of health, you may have noticed how integrated they are to each other in your own life. When I address one area, I feel an impact on many others. For example, when I focus on improving my physical wellness and start working out more often, I affect my emotional and social wellness areas. The next chapter focuses on the Recovery Phase. As already noted, our areas of wellness are a large part of recovery. As we use actions impacting each wellness area, we create recovery spaces for ourselves.

Chapter Seven

Building Our Recovery Formulas

"The wise rest at least as hard as they work."
—Mokokoma Mokhonoana

Now, you might be wondering why a book on burnout recovery would address the phase of Recovery in one of the book's last chapters. You may be thinking this because the Recovery Phase is undoubtedly the most important one in the model. But it is not. First, all three phases work together to create a resilient person to burnout. Not one phase can fully happen without the other two. Second, I believe the Observation and Preparation Phases are more critical in addressing your burnout and supporting you when you have moved beyond it. No one can overcome the feelings of burnout until they have identified what they are experiencing as burnout. Recognizing Burn Events is an essential first step; the second is preparing for them. The Preparation Phase supports us in finding small ways to be ready for those feelings of overwhelm; it also creates the time and space for recovery activities.

So far, we have covered how to identify your burnout and Burn Events, how to prepare for times of stress and overwhelm, and the six areas of wellness you need to be mindful of in all three phases. Now we can dig into how we create recovery in our lives. That is through building your Recovery Formulas.

But I am getting a little ahead of myself because we still need to define how you will know you have reached recovery. This looks slightly different for every person, as we all have different recovery needs. My definition is: that I show up as my happiest, healthiest self where ever I go. My happiest, healthiest self can also vary day by day. Because some days I am in a foul mood, and I struggle to get out of that emotional place, and that's okay. In general though, when I am my happiest, healthiest self, I wake up each morning excited about the day; I feel connected and energized by my work, I smile more and complain less. In short, I am the opposite of the worst version of myself that I experience when I am in burnout.

Let's do a reflection exercise to help you identify how you look, feel, and act when you are in your recovery space. After reading this, I want you to close your eyes and take as much time as you need to visualize. You may want to write it down. Then when you finish come back here.

Future Self Reflection

I have a magic wand that works across the land and oceans to impact you where you are sitting today. When I wave my magic wand, you will be whisked away to one year in the future. But something has changed. You are no longer experiencing the burdens of burnout, and you are living your perfect day. Picture that day in your mind from the moment you wake up to the moment you fall asleep feeling so happy and grateful. What do your routines look like? Where do you live? Who is there with you? What are you doing for a living? Do you have hobbies? Focus on all the details. I will see you back here soon.

Reflection Debrief

Welcome back! I wish to be there with you and hear about your perfect day. You can always drop me a DM on social media @drkatesteiner. Here's the deal, your perfect day is you are in burnout recovery. You enjoyed doing the things throughout the day that are pieces to your recovery formulas. That morning routine you pictured, yep, that's something you are craving for recovery. Hear me (read me) now. I am not saying you should jump into recreating your perfect day tomorrow. I am saying some of the things you saw on your perfect day that you can slowly add to your life now. What if you woke up a few minutes earlier to have that mindful moment with your first cup of coffee? Think back on your perfect day. What specifically were things you did to combat feelings of stress?

Recovery Formulas

Now, let's talk about developing your Recovery Formulas. I have a few different recovery formulas; I use formulas for daily recovery. I have formulas that I use for weekly recovery. And then, I have formulas that I use throughout the year for more substantial recovery when I need a more extended break from work and everyday life. I call them vacation recovery formulas. When they think about rest and recovery, most people only think about what they do on the weekend, during a holiday, or on vacation. If you only allow recovery during those times, you will always wear out before you get there. This is why I want you to start with Daily Recovery Formulas.

Daily recovery formulas help you maintain energy through Burn Events and create space for decompression time. For me, it often includes things like music, no interruptions, and some time and space to reflect on my own. Having a solo dance party is a good example of my daily recovery formulas. Music + No Interruptions + Movement = Dance Party = Recovery.

With this book, you've already started the reflection process to build your daily recovery formulas. In Chapter Six, you had the opportunity to reflect on ways to positively impact each wellness area. Your desire to address your sleep schedule can be built into a Recovery Formula by creating an unwinding routine for yourself. It could be Reflection/Prayer + Soft Music + Weighted Blanket = Bedtime = Recovery. You may have noticed that you impact multiple wellness areas when building a Recovery Formula.

Your Weekly Recovery Formulas are what you will implement when you have a day off and a little more downtime. What's that? You say you don't have downtime because you have too many things to do during those days off.

Well, here's the harsh truth: you are responsible for all the busyness in your life. And… You can create the space for recovery. So back to our Weekly Recovery Formulas. I need people and human interaction as part of my Weekly formula. People outside of a Zoom meeting and beyond my partner in the house since I work from home. I get this interaction and impact my business simultaneously by joining a networking group and attending the weekly meetings. It may also come from hanging out socially with friends. Then there are some weeks when I need a full day of lounging around and reading in my hammock or watching Hallmark movies while baking sourdough bread. The required activity depends on the week I have experienced, which may change, but I always have slated the time to recover, usually on a Saturday or Sunday for at least a few hours, if not an entire day.

Vacation Recovery

Picture your last vacation. Was it restful? Did you return home feeling rejuvenated? Or did you feel more tired than when you left? Sometimes these times away can wear us down more than support us in recovering. Partly because we were so overwhelmed when we went, there was no way a four-day trip could give you enough rest to recover from six months of Burn Events. The other challenge is that we are not intentional about what we do on those vacations. Meaning we do not approach it by seeking rest and rejuvenation. We pack in every possible activity we can; we rise early and stay up late so we don't miss a moment of our time away. If you are using this time for recovery, you must be mindful of a few things. Think about where and whom you are going with, and do they have similar expectations for the trip as you? Then think about what you need while on that vacation to help you relax.

My formula for Vacation Recovery looks like Water + Sunlight + Nature + Rest = Recovery. You will most likely find me on a beach chair next to the ocean with an umbrella giving me shade, with a book in my lap and a drink in my hand. And I will be on the beach all day. I have learned that I need to travel with people who enjoy hanging out with me on the beach or don't mind going off alone for a little while. I have friends who would be bored silly and have a much more active vacation recovery formula. I also take trips that I know will not equal rest, so I don't include them in my overall recovery plan. Instead, I plan ways to recover from them as Burn Events when I return home, probably with a Hallmark movie day.

I wonder if you struggle with doing nothing. When was the last time that you rested, truly rested? We tend to have a hard time achieving recovery because the hustle culture of our world has misinformed us that rest and recovery are equivalent to being lazy. When we "do nothing," we are being very productive. Consider any fitness training program; it always includes recovery periods when done well. Your body, mind, and soul need breaks from the nonstop action that comes with the hustle mindset. If the thought of creating Recovery Formulas to create spaces of rest makes you uncomfortable, that's normal; change initially feels weird. You can get there by taking those small micro-steps, incorporating short rest periods into your day, then your week, and throughout the year.

Let's try it together right now. I want you to set a timer for 2 – 5 minutes. Do you have it ready? Great! If music helps you, I recommend using a song without lyrics that will help you relax or reflect. No remove yourself from other distractions, put the phone on, do not disturb, step away from your computer. Take a nice deep breath and slowly exhale while counting to five when you start your timer. Close your eyes and let your thoughts flow; try not to place judgment on them or dig into them too much; let them come and go. When your timer goes off, take another deep breath, once again exhaling slowly as you count to five.

Okay, now give it a try; I'm here cheering you on!

Welcome back! So... How do you feel? You just meditated. You just now rested your mind and body. Just now, you paused the busyness. Right then, you gave yourself a moment of recovery. And it only took a few minutes. What might it feel like to create that space several times throughout the day? What might you experience if you increased it to 20 minutes during a day off from work? Remember, start with the micro-steps because they can create a huge impact.

I have introduced the types of Recovery Formulas you need, and now I will speak on what you should include as the building blocks. There are four themes that I recommend everyone uses to build their Recovery Formulas; Play, Gratitude, the Comfort List, and Grounding Exercises.

Play

We do not play nearly enough as adults. Somewhere along the way in growing, we get to be too serious. For me, it happened around the age of 12 or 13. I remember feeling thankful because I had a younger sister and could still play Barbies with her. Or my friends and I would sneak playing Barbies. Something that we vowed never to tell anyone else at school. I'm sad now thinking about that, that the opinions of others kept me from an activity that brought me joy. I was unkind to my sister because I felt that being a grown-up meant that you had to be more serious, and being serious meant that you stopped playing. So, I stopped playing; then, as an adult, I found ways to bring play back into my life, like my dance parties, a group fitness class, game nights with friends, or getting out on the water on a paddleboard.

Play is how children learn and is a way to learn new things. Play increases our creativity, develops our problem-solving skills, and reduces stress. You want to find ways to incorporate play into your life. How do you know something you are doing is play? I like to use the 7 Properties of Play by Dr. Stuart Brown to identify play. Dr. Brown says that for human beings, "play lies at the core of creativity and innovation. Without it, life would hardly be worth living."

7 Properties of Play

Purposelessness: Play is apparently purposeless and seems to happen without guided direction. Remember, the play has a purpose and a significant impact because you reduce stress, learn, and enhance your creativity.

Voluntary: Play is voluntary. You should never be volun-told. Play is always something that you enter into entirely on your own. It has no obligatory aspect. It is never something you 'have' to do.

Inherent Attraction: Play is fun and makes us feel good. When you see other people being playful, you want to join in and be playful with them.

Freedom From Time: Play releases us from the construct of time. Time can speed up or slow down.

Diminished Consciousness of Self: Play creates a space where we do not worry about what other people think about us. By now you know I am a big fan of a dance party, which is probably my most prominent form of play. For me, whenever a good song is playing, it's a good time to dance, even down the grocery store aisle. I also dance in the grocery stores. If the music is good, and I need to move it out, I will do that. I'm in my zone. I'm in my own little dance space. I only care about being in that moment.

Improvisational Potential: Play involves spontaneous potential, the idea that anything can happen. I love the improv rule, "yes, and" where to keep the act going, you can only say yes to whatever has been presented, and then you add to it. I love using this to brainstorm with others when we are stuck finding a solution to a problem. This opens the door to being more creative because nothing is off the table.

Continuation Desire: Play produces the desire to continue playing. Once you start playing, you may not want to stop. Ever get the giggles in a meeting? It can be hard to stop if you are like me and have a colleague who has a knowing glance across the table.

There are lots of different ways that we can still play as adults. You can use a coloring book, play games on your phone, enjoy the sense of humor of a friend, play with your kids or pets, or stop at a playground and try the swings. Start with activities that achieve the first two properties, apparent purposelessness and voluntary. What are some of the things you already do in your life that can be defined as Play?

Gratitude

Gratitude is a positive emotion, and when you train your brain to feel a positive emotion over a negative, it positively impacts your mental well-being. Gratitude is not ignoring any painful feelings or experiences you have, though; it is more about honoring all of your emotions and experiences. Some you can find grace in them, and others you may not. We are healthier mentally and emotionally when we experience our feelings rather than ignoring or pushing them away. When you practice gratitude, you help rewire your brain to have a different emotional response to look for the grace in each experience. And this helps build resilience. Here are five ways that you can add Gratitude to your Recovery Formulas.

Start and end each day with Gratitude. This doesn't have to be a fancy practice. It can be as simple as stating, "I am grateful for waking" and "I am grateful for this one thing today." You can include it as part of a journaling practice or use a Post-it note reminder on the bathroom mirror.

Shift apologies to Gratitude. Instead of apologizing, especially for something you cannot control, like traffic, offer grace instead. For example, once in a workspace, we had sent students the wrong paperwork in an email to be filled out and brought with them. When they arrived, instead of apologizing for the confusion, I said to each, "Thank you for being prepared; the paperwork has changed, so we will need you to fill these out instead." The gratitude helped ease any annoyance they may have felt in filling out the second set of paperwork.

Be authentic in your Gratitude. You don't want to force it. If you start by being thankful to have coffee each morning, then go with that. If this is all new to you, start small. Offer grace for the things you naturally think of, like your family, pets, sunshine, etc.

Your gratitude list may be shorter to start, and then you will build on it. Try starting with things that gave you a sense of accomplishment in the day. Remember, what you are grateful for will not match other people's gratitude around you.

The Silver Lining Question. When an outside event impacts you, ask, "What are the silver linings here?" For example, when my partner and I moved into our house, we encountered continuous things that should have been repaired years prior, and it was frustrating. One of the worst moments was when our lower level flooded a second time just a few weeks after everything was repaired. The brand-new floors were ruined once again. When I discovered the water, I was livid, just beyond pissed. Then I reminded myself that we have insurance for a reason. After hiring a different company to assess the damage and clean up our space, we found that several walls had mold in them (this wasn't caught during the first flood); we worked with our excellent contractor and now have a remolded space that would have taken years to do if the flood had not occurred. Seek out the silver linings.

Gratitude is not a magic bullet. Practicing gratitude will help you shift your thoughts and emotions in a more positive direction, but it's not meant to be a solo act. It should be a part of your mental wellness practice. It can enhance the work that you are doing with a counselor, therapist, or coach. It can help ground you when negative emotions are threatening to take over. Gratitude is essential to your wellness puzzle, but you must use additional building blocks to make your Recovery Formulas whole.

Your Comfort List

Another building block for your Recovery Formula is your Comfort List. The Comfort List lists items, activities, interactions, people, and things that bring you calm, joy, a sense of peace or comfort, and warmth. Think about how you might comfort a friend or upset child. Your Comfort List comprises predetermined things that will comfort you when upset or overwhelmed. Think of it as your self-soothing toolbox. For example, some of the things on my Comfort List are mac and cheese. It is my number one comfort item and why I avoid any type of restrictive eating plan that removes all the foods that brought me joy. I also include a cup of tea, a nice cozy sweater, fuzzy socks, Hallmark movies, a hug from someone I care about, and time in my hammock on a warm summer day.

I have Comfort Lists for each season. I need different things to comfort me based on the weather and how I feel during each season. I tend to feel more sadness in the winter; my comfort list changes to help address that by adding reality tv to the mix because I find humor and gratitude in watching other people's lives. I want to spend more time outside and in the sun during the summer, so my Comfort List shifts to include activities like hammock time, paddle boarding, and walking around my neighborhood.

Take a break from reading right now and start your Comfort List. What are some of the things that you are already doing in your life to provide comfort? What are things you used to do that you would like to bring back into your life? You will want to come back to reflecting on your Comfort List often, as you will find that what you need for comfort will change as you continue to develop your response to Burnout and Burn Events.

Grounding Exercises

A final building block for your Recovery Formula is using a Grounding exercise. These are incredibly important because they help us ground down when we are in a heightened stress state. When we are stressed, we lose our ability to make rational decisions because our frontal cortex goes offline. In those moments, our amygdala takes over. Because our brain wants to keep us safe, we go into fight, flight, or freeze mode. When we ground ourselves with grounding exercises, we tell our physical body that we are safe and that our frontal cortex can resume decision-making. Grounding exercises are short; they are meant to act quickly to ease anxiety. They are exercises that you can use anywhere. Here are three that I use often.

The 5, 4, 3, 2, 1 Method

This is one of my favorite techniques. This method utilizes all five of your senses and the space around you.

Take a nice big deep breath, and slowly exhale.

Name five things you can see.

Name four things you can touch.

Name three things you can hear.

Name two things you can smell.

Name one thing you can taste.

Take one more nice deep breath filling your entire chest and belly with air, and exhale slowly.

You can repeat the steps as many times as needed until you feel the stress in your body release, your heart rate slow, and your breathing relaxes. While you are naming the things you see, touch, hear, smell, and taste, you also want to describe each of the items in your mind, using as many details as you can. As if you were explaining it to someone who couldn't see those things or someone who couldn't smell or taste those things.

Counting Your Breaths

Breathing techniques and breathwork also help us ground back into our bodies. Taking ten slow, deep breaths is a straightforward yet effective way to start a grounding practice.

While focusing your attention on each inhale and exhale.

As you inhale, focus on taking the biggest, longest breath you can.

As you exhale, say the number you're on, counting backward from 10 to one.

Breath in
Exhale 10

Breath in
Exhale 9

Breath in
Exhale 8

Breath in
Exhale 7

Breath in
Exhale 6

Breath in
Exhale 5

Breath in
Exhale 4

Breath in
Exhale 3

Breath in
Exhale 2

Breath in
Exhale 1

You can continue by then counting back up from one to 10. This reduces your stress response, helps lower your blood pressure, and grounds you into the earth to calm your body and nervous system.

Box Breathing

The last Grounding Exercise that I will introduce here is box breathing. This is another breathing technique that you implement anywhere. It is a counted breath where you inhale for four counts, hold for four accounts, exhale for four counts, and hold again for four counts. As you breathe, it helps to picture a box or draw a box, like the one below.

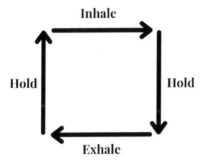

You will repeat the counted breath at least three times. I find that five or six-box breaths work best for me. Try each of these Grounding Exercises, and you may find that one works better for you than the others.

Now you have several building blocks that you can use to create your Recovery Formulas. You may decide to take a recovery break as part of your lunch hour, and during that time, you will include something from Your Comfort List and a Grounding Exercise. Maybe weekly, you have Playtime and Comfort List time for recovery. How might you create an entire vacation around Play and Grounding Exercises?

I addressed this some above, but I am often asked this question. "How do you make time for recovery when you already have so many other things going on?" My answer is always the same you have the time. You've just filled it with other things, tasks, and expectations. You have to prioritize your recovery time. Remember that the most crucial person in your life is YOU. If you are not here, then nothing else exists. It is essential to schedule and prioritize the time you need for rest and recovery for your health.

In Closing

"Take time today to pause, to linger, to quiet the noise, and remember that your worth is not measured by your productivity."
—A Life in Progress

We have traveled from Feeling Crispy through the Steiner Self-Reflection Sustainability and Wellness Model in Observation, Preparation, and Recovery. Now we've reached the end of the book, but not the end of your journey. You must think about this as a process or a journey. Our approach to Burnout Recovery is never really finished as we encounter new Burn Events and Recovery Formula building blocks; our process will evolve and change with us as we continue to live.

My Burnout Recovery journey started slowly, with those small micro-steps. Creating that habits that now support me every day. We cannot avoid Burnout, but we do not have to stay stuck there either. We can approach our Burn Events differently through Observation, Preparation, and Recovery in a more resilient way.

I hope this book will continue to be a resource you return to as you continue your journey. Thank you for joining me on these pages, and know I am committed to being a constant resource for you in this space.

For more resources, check out: www.liftwellnessconsulting.com/FeelingCrispy.

Dr. Kate Steiner is a Burnout Recovery expert, coach, consultant, and founder of LIFT Wellness Consulting.

She supports her clients from burnout to recovery by developing a self-reflective plan that identifies and prepares for burn events by addressing all areas of wellness. Holding A Master of Counseling and a Ph.D. in Counselor Education and Supervision, her practice is grounded in the research-based Steiner Self-Reflective Sustainability and Wellness (SSRSW) model, published in the Oracle Research Journal. This model stems from her own experience with burnout; she refers back to being the worst version of herself during that time. She has been a researcher in wellness and burnout for over 17 years. Her work has been published in consumer outlets including, The LIST, Authority Magazine, Thrive Global, Daytime Blue Ridge (NBC), WTTA (NBC) Bloom TV, FOX Good Day Washington, and myfitnesspal, and industry publications, Essentials, and Perspectives Magazine.

She hosts The From Burnout to Recovery Show with Dr. Kate. Her mission is to end the burnout cycle for professionals to live happier, healthier lives.

References

Brown, S. L. (2009). *Play: How it shapes the brain, opens the imagination, and invigorates the soul.* Penguin.

Maslach, C., Jackson, S.E., & Leiter, M.P. (1996) *Maslach Burnout Inventory Manual, 3ʳᵈ Edition,* Menlo Park, CA: Mind Garden, Inc.

Maslach, C., & Leiter, M. P. (1997). *The truth about burnout: How organizations cause personal stress and what to do about it.* San Francisco: Jossey-Bass.

Steiner, K. D. (2017). *Anchor Down: A Grounded Theory Study of Sustaining Careers in the Fraternity/Sorority Advising Profession*

Made in the USA
Middletown, DE
29 October 2023

41432593R00049